D1061348

For Shane, Miranda, Helena and Joseph S.T.
For Jane, Gillian, Margaret and Evelyn C.F.

Takwe nzila pe itayi kumunzi.
There is no path that does not lead to a home.
(Tonga proverb)

WHO MADE ME?

Text copyright © 2000 Shirley Tulloch
Illustrations copyright © 2000 Cathie Felstead
This edition copyright © 2000 Lion Publishing

The moral rights of the author and illustrator
have been asserted

Except for brief quotations in critical articles or reviews, no part of this book
may be reproduced in any manner without prior written permission from the publisher.
Write to: Permissions, Augsburg Fortress, Box 1209, Minneapolis, MN 55440.

First Augsburg Books edition. Originally published as Who Made Me?
copyright © 1998 Lion Publishing plc., Sandy Lane West, Oxford, England.

Library of Congress Cataloging in Publication Data
ISBN 0-8066-4045-6 (alk. paper)
AF 9-4045

First edition 2000

10 9 8 7 6 5 4 3 2 1 0

Who Made Me?

Shirley Tulloch
Illustrated by Cathie Felstead

Augsburg
MINNEAPOLIS

Zanele lived in a quiet little village.
It was a place where the sun always shone
brightly and the stars twinkled like
thousands of diamonds. Night was as
beautiful as day where Zanele lived.

Zanele had one very important question. "WHO MADE ME?" she asked herself every night as she stared up at the silver moon.

Now Zanele had seven very special friends, and she was certain that one of them would be able to answer her question. Early one morning, as the sun was rising, she began her journey. "I'll ask Lion; he'll be able to tell me," she said, skipping towards his den.

"Who made you?" growled Lion. "It was someone just like me. Someone very powerful and courageous. A bit like a king, I suppose."

"Mmm, that sounds correct," thought Zanele. "I'll ask Giraffe too. She will have a good answer."

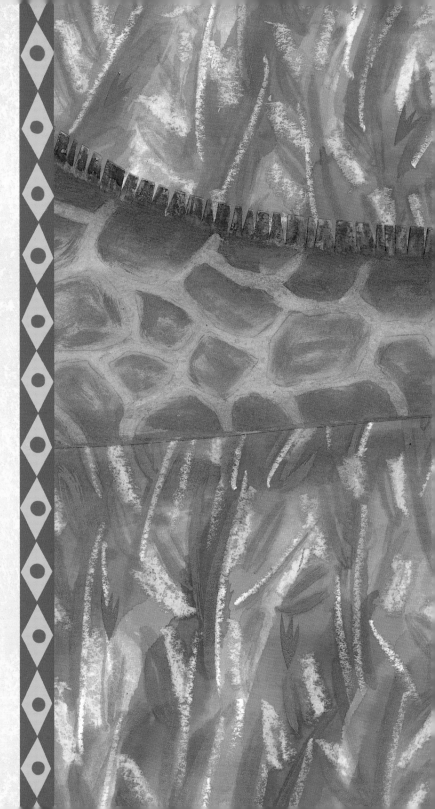

"Who made you?" Giraffe mumbled as she chewed leaves from the top of the tallest tree. "It was someone just like me. Someone very gentle and extremely kind. Shall I pass you one of these juicy leaves? They're delicious."

"No," laughed Zanele, "but thank you for your answer."

She was still staring up at the enormous giraffe when Baboon swung down from the lowest branch and landed at Zanele's feet. She asked him the important question.

"Who made you?" chuckled Baboon, "Well, that's easy. It was someone just like me. Someone who is always close to you and often makes you laugh!"

"I like that answer!" Zanele smiled as she continued her journey.

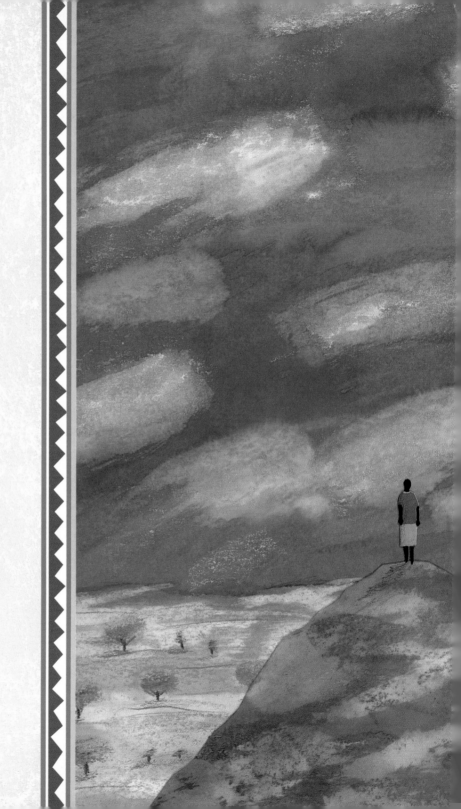

It was almost midday and Zanele was very hot as she climbed to the top of a hill. She wanted to feel the cool breeze on her face. As she was looking at a little cloud no bigger than the size of a hand, she saw another friend, the big black eagle.

"Who made you?" cried Eagle after Zanele had asked the question. "It was someone just like me." The eagle soared into the sky and called, "Someone who can see and understand everything." Then she swooped low, just above Zanele's head, and added, "Someone who gives you surprises!"

Zanele watched Eagle fly away until she was just a tiny dot in the sky.

Later that afternoon, down in the valley, Zanele saw Zebra trotting along a dusty road. "Wait for me, I have a question for you. Who made me?" she shouted.

"Who made you?" Zebra paused, flicked his tail and twitched his ears. "It was someone just like me. Someone very special. Can you see my family over there in those bushes? Well each one of us is very different. No two zebras have the same stripes. You won"t find another one like me!"

"That's amazing," thought Zanele.

It was evening and the sun was just beginning to sink behind the hills when Zanele heard a beautiful sound. It was the song of a little bird, the honey-guide. "Follow me," sang the little bird.

Zanele ran after the honey-guide until she was out of breath. Suddenly, in the thickest part of the bush, they stopped. Zanele could hear the buzzing of bees, and she knew exactly what to do. When the honey-guide leads you to a bees' nest, you must share the honey with her.

As Zanele broke the honeycomb, the little bird perched on her shoulder and they both enjoyed the sweetest treat.

Licking the honey from her lips, Zanele asked the question.

"Who made you?" sang Honey-guide. "It was someone just like me. Someone who leads you to good things. Someone who shares their gifts."

anele was feeling tired as she made her way back home. The moon and stars were just beginning to appear as she approached her village. Suddenly a voice from the shadows of the trees trumpeted, "Where have you been all day? I was worried about you." It was Elephant. Zanele was so pleased that she had found the last of her friends.

"I have been trying to find the answer to a very important question," she explained. "I want to know who made me."

Elephant stood still for a long time. Eventually, she raised her trunk into the air and then spoke very softly:"Who made you? It was someone just like me. Someone strong and very wise. Someone who will never forget you."

Zanele nodded and then sighed. "I have had seven good answers to my question, but which one is correct?"

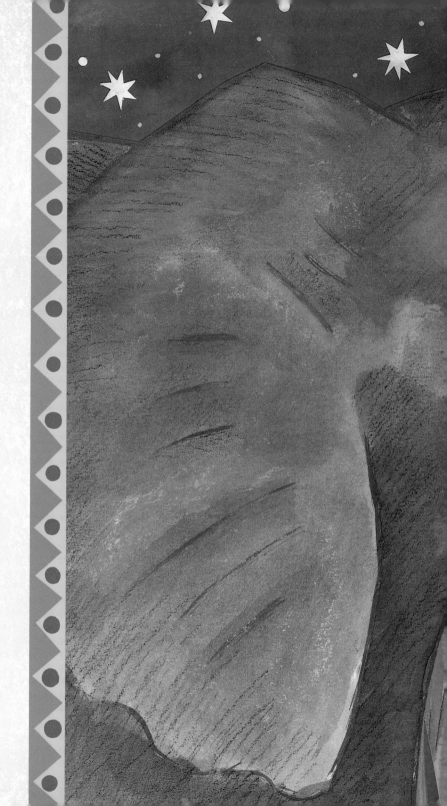

"Ah," said Elephant, "sometimes there *are* seven answers to one question, you know."

"Seven answers?" puzzled Zanele.

"Yes, let me explain . . ." and Elephant swung her trunk around the little girl's waist and lifted her up carefully to whisper in her ear. Then she placed her softly back on the ground.

Zanele smiled. "Now I know who made me.

"Someone powerful and courageous, like Lion.

"Someone gentle and kind, like Giraffe.

"Someone close to me who makes me laugh, like Baboon.

"Someone who can see and understand everything, like Eagle.

"Someone very special, like Zebra.

"Someone who leads me to good things, like Honey-guide.

"Someone strong and very wise, who never forgets me, like you, Elephant."

As the great elephant marched off into the darkness, Zanele felt very happy that her question had been answered at last. She looked up at the beautiful night sky. It was shimmering with the silver of moon and stars.